Copyright © 2012 by Habitat for Humanity of the Chesapeake Interfaith Coalition

All rights reserved. No part of this book may be reproduced or transmitted in any form or by any means, electronic or mechanical, including photocopy, recording, or any information storage and retrieval system, without prior permission from the publisher (except by reviewers who may quote brief passages).

Printed in the United States of America

First Edition

Cover and interior design: Mary Henkels
Cover art: Diana, age 13

Printed in the United States of America

ISBN: 978-1-934074-74-9

Published by Apprentice House
The Future of Publishing…Today!

Apprentice House
Communication Department
Loyola University Maryland
450 N. Charles Street
Baltimore, MD 21210

410.617.5265
410.617.2198 (fax)
www.ApprenticeHouse.com
info@ApprenticeHouse.com

Peace by Piece

All proceeds go to
Habitat for Humanity of the Chesapeake's
Interfaith-sponsored homes.

Habitat for Humanity!!

Ana, age 8

What is Habitat for Humanity?

As an affiliate of Habitat for Humanity International, Habitat for Humanity of the Chesapeake's mission is to work with God and people of all faiths to build safe, decent affordable houses. Partners work together with families in need and community members to eliminate poverty housing and help revitalize communities.

The affiliate's mission statement is: *Putting faith into action, Habitat for Humanity of the Chesapeake brings people together to build decent, affordable homes that change lives, empower families and strengthen communities.*

Habitat for Humanity of the Chesapeake is located in Maryland and serves Anne Arundel County, Baltimore City, Baltimore County and Howard County. To learn more about this affiliate visit www.habitatchesapeake.org for information. To learn more about Habitat for Humanity International or to find an affiliate in your area, visit www.habitat.org.

Peace by Piece

The *Peace by Piece* initiative does just that—we advocate for *peace* one *piece* at a time. We work to involve Christian, Islamic and Jewish partners in the Interfaith Volunteer Corps working side by side with community residents and the future homeowners. The *Peace by Piece* partners began in 2007-2008 by completing two homes in Baltimore. In addition to building homes, *Peace by Piece* partners work to build bridges of understanding. This book includes children in that effort by helping all of us learn from the wisdom of their faith.

Your contribution in purchasing this book will help to continue the work of the Interfaith Volunteer Corps with Habitat for Humanity of the Chesapeake. Thank you.

Sami
10

✡ Sami, age 10

About the Book
what we did...

The authors of the book are Jewish, Christian, or Muslim children from ages 5 to 17. We at Habitat for Humanity of the Chesapeake visited all of these boys and girls and asked them to draw pictures of what they thought about certain elements of their own religion. The only instruction they were given was to answer through pictures the questions we provided. These thought provoking questions included:

Who is God? God is... God is like...
What does God teach us about shelter?
What does God teach us about helping the poor?
What does God teach us about caring for the earth?
What does God teach us about being a family?
How are we connected to other people who are different than us?

The children were given only these questions and no other outside input to influence their responses. What they drew is purely their own genuine thoughts and ideas. These pictures represent the opinions and interpretations of each child and are their way of expressing themselves. The drawings give each child the opportunity to speak to us through his or her pictures and provide insight as to how they view their own faith. It is their voice and their chance to be heard.

This book will introduce other children to different religions so that they may be able to see some of the similarities and differences among them. We hope that the children will be able to see both the uniqueness of each picture and the uncanny ability to relate to those who are different from themselves. Ultimately, this is our attempt to introduce the children to interfaith activities and dialogue at an early age, in the hope that they will become open minded and accepting individuals.

Who is God?

Yashinah, age 10

Diana, age 13, from an Interfaith family

✝ Caleb, age 8

moon is by God

☾★Precious, age 7

ALLAH is God He made The Sun

☾★Precious, age 7

✡ Edwin, age 9

☪ Jocelyn, age 8

✡ Hannah, age 9

✝ Alex, age 9

What does God teach us about shelter?

✝ Will, Age 8

✡ Shira, age 9

✡ David, Age 5

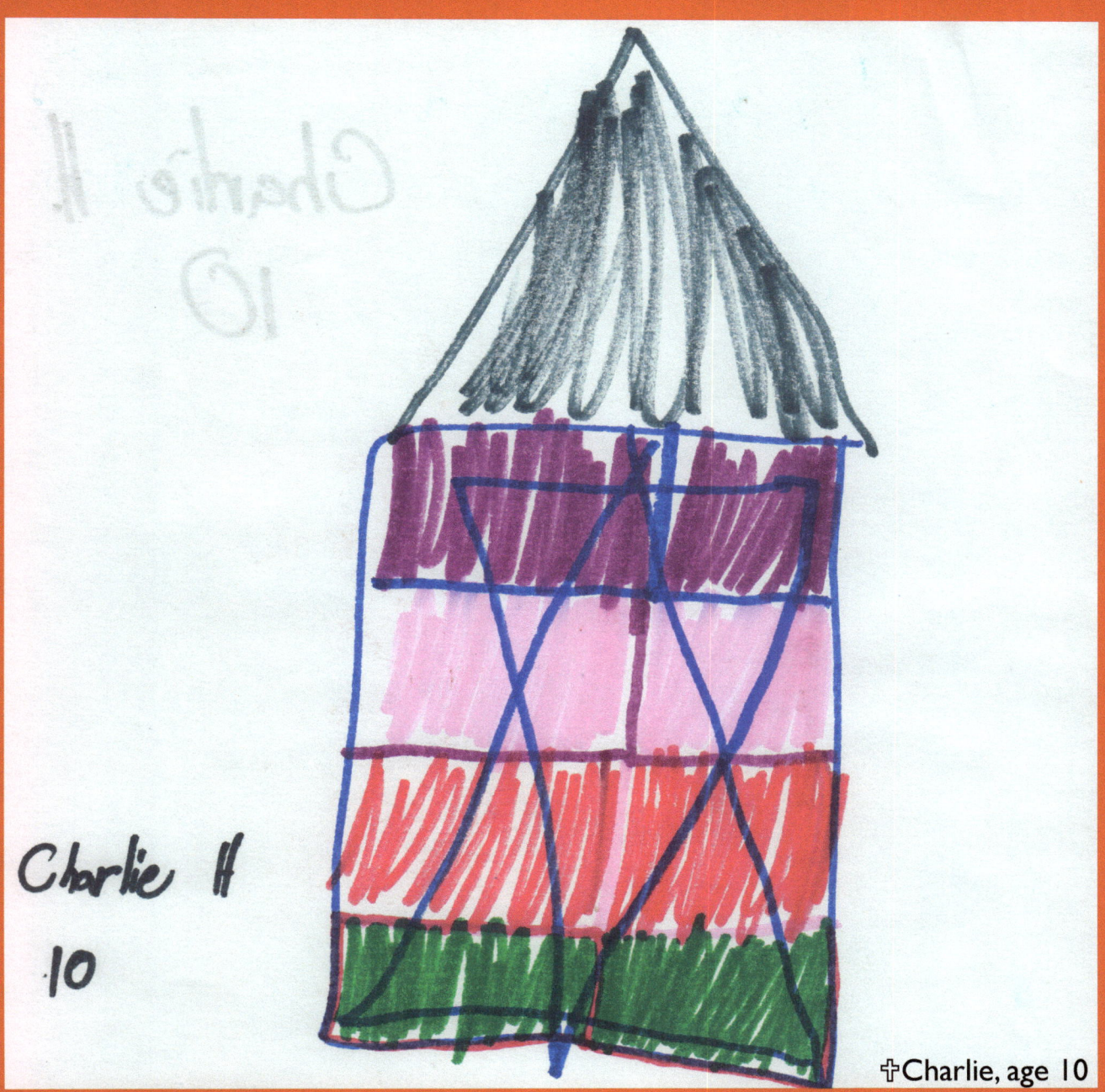

☦Charlie, age 10

Allah teaches us about shelter by building homes for people who don't have a home.

☪ Anonymous

Danny, age 6

✝ Wesley, age 9

What does God teach us about helping the poor?

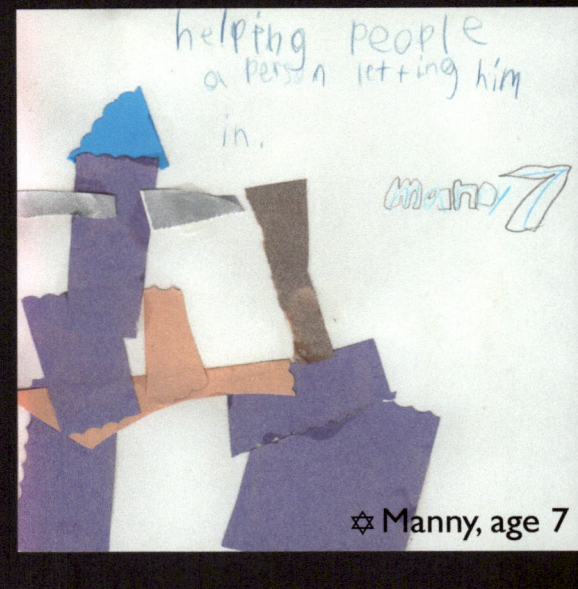

Manny, age 7

Joan, age 8

helping people   Manny. 7
One good deed leeds to another good deed

Manny, age 7

✝ Pierre, age 8

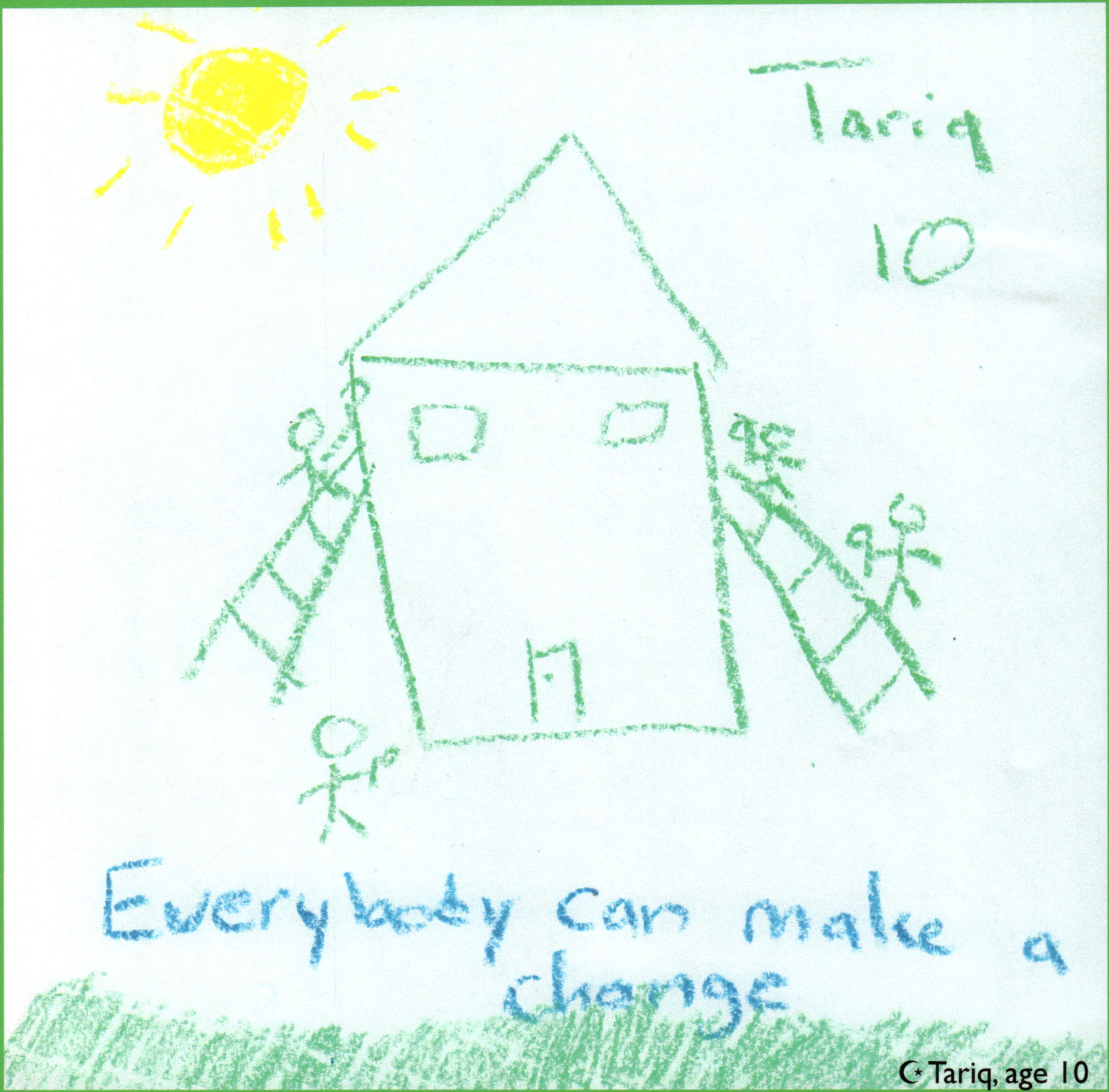

Tariq, age 10

✝Nonnie, age 7

✝Campbell, age 9

✝Danielle, age 6

✝ T.J. age 9

✝ Peyton, age 8

✡Shoshana, age 9

✡ Joan, age 8

†Yasmine, age 8

Jonathan, age 8

"God teaches us about helping the poor by how they don't have as much great thing we do. We give money to the poor. We should always think about the poor."

✡Hailey, age 10

What does God teach us about caring for the earth?

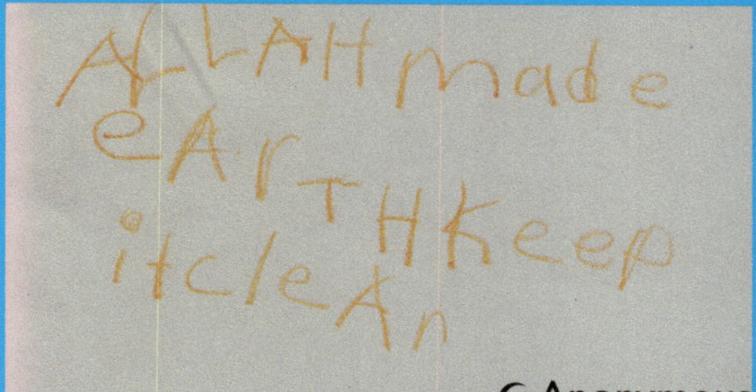

ALLAH made eARTH keep it cleAn

☪ Anonymous

☪ Taufeeq, age 14

✝ Conner, age 9

✝ Charlotte, age 8

Evie, age 7

✝ Hunter, age 8

Allah tells us to take care of the Earth by watering plants.

☪ Yaminah, age 10

Tariq 10

☪ Tariq, age 10

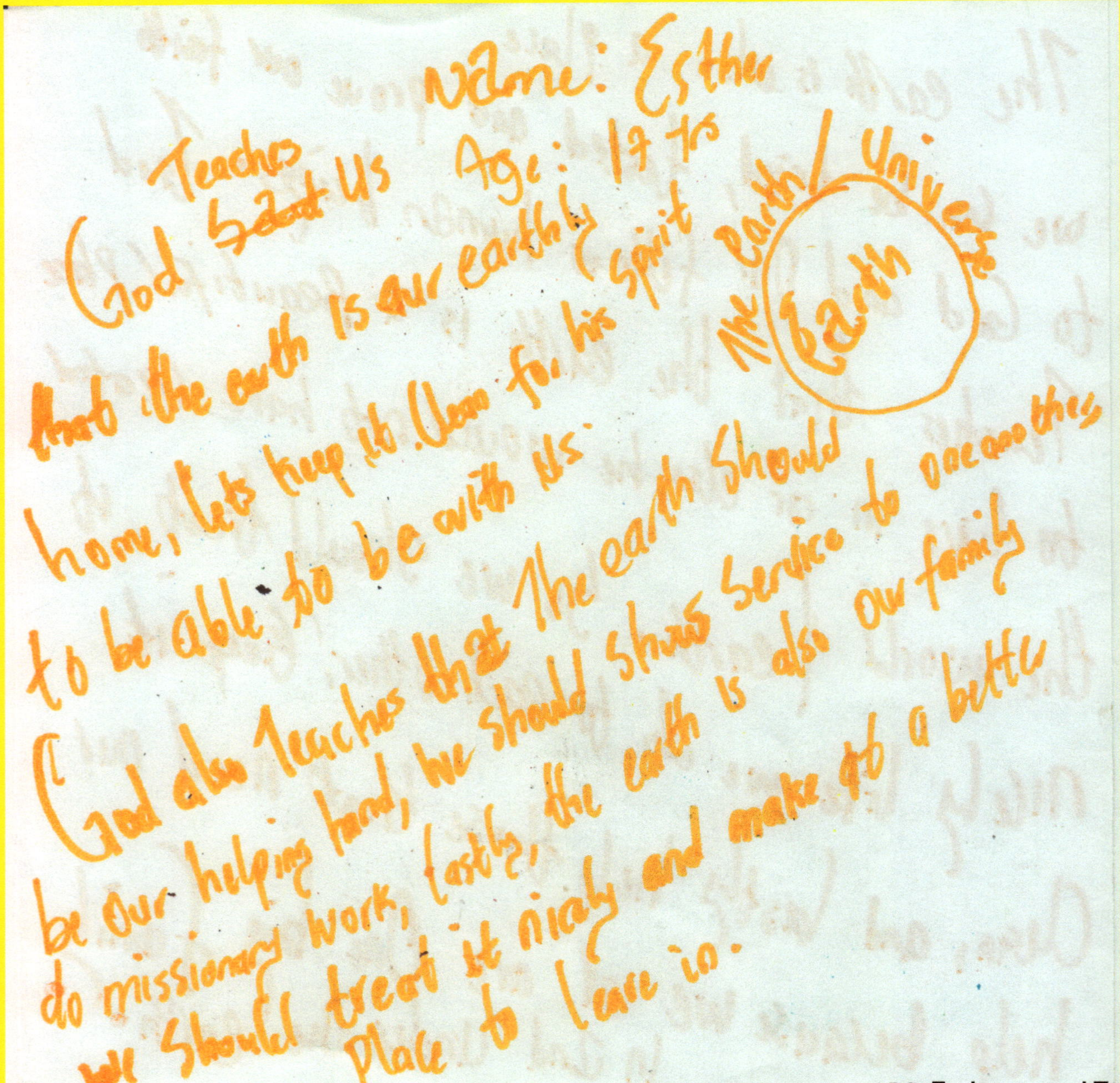

Name: Esther
Age: 17 yrs

Teaches

God taught us that the earth is our earthly home, let's keep it clean for his spirit to be able to be with us.

The Earth / Universe

Earth

God also Teaches that The earth should be our helping hand, We should show Service to one another, do missionary work, Lastly, the earth is also our family we should treat it nicely and make it a better place to live in.

LDS Esther, age 17

The earth is also a place we can be tried, tested and prove our faith to God and our fellow human beings. God teaches that the earth is a beautiful place to live in or else he would not have created the world / earth. So we should treat it nicely like we do to each other. Keep it clean, and lastly help those that need our help because we all are one big family in 2nd under the earth.

LDS Esther, age 17

What does God teach us about being a family?

We come together
✝ Kyle, age 14

✝ Kyle, age 14

How are we connected to people who are different than us?

✝Hunter, age 8

"Everyone's Important. In Different way's!?." Age = 9
By Aminah

Habitat

©Aminah, age 9

☪ Tresleen, age 6

Allah teaches us to stay close to our family and never apart.

☪ Yaminah, age 10

Happy family

☪ Ameen, age 10

✝ Alexandra, age 8

"But We Are All the Same, We all think about God!"

☾ Aminah, age 9

What God Teaches us

It's I

✝ Erin, age 10

✝ David, age 8

Why We Care For and Help Others

Ethan, age 11

Christian Response

In Christianity, we are called to follow Jesus. He tells us that whenever we reach out to others who are hungry, need clothing or shelter, are in prison or are sick, we reach out to Him. So, we know we are called to reach out to the poor. When asked what is the greatest commandment, Jesus said, "To love your neighbor as yourself." So, we try to live our lives loving our neighbors. The prophets also told us about God's vision for a world of peace and equality. We see it as our responsibility to help build that world!

Muslim Response

Islam teaches its followers to help and care for others, and to give to people who are in need of assistance. Giving help to others is not voluntary. All Muslims give annual zakat, or charity, to the poor. How much money a Muslim must give is calculated based on a percentage of their income. Muslims are also encouraged to give charity to those in need at all times, with a particular emphasis on helping the poor, widows, and orphans. Islam also teaches people to be friendly and kind to their neighbors and strangers. Smiling and greeting people is even considered a "good deed!"

Jewish Response

A core Jewish value is the idea of Tzedakah, literally "righteousness." Tzedakah is commonly used to mean charitable giving or service, showing that helping others is a righteous action. Other elements of a Jewish person's obligations include visiting the sick, feeding the hungry, and comforting mourners. The ancient Rabbis (teachers) clearly extended the obligation to help those in need beyond the Jewish community. The commandment to care for the poor, the widow, and the orphan is found more times than any other in the Torah.

Places We Worship

Christian Response

The sanctuary is a place where worship services are held in the Christian tradition. It often has an altar in front where you find candles (representing the light of Jesus) and the communion elements (bread and wine). Sunday worship usually involves a choir, a sermon, singing hymns and partaking of communion. Some sanctuaries are very formal with pews and lecterns or pulpits that have the minister above the people. Some are very informal with moveable chairs and a communion table placed in the middle of the people. All are considered holy places where Christians gather to worship and praise God. Worship can also happen anywhere, and many see outdoors as God's sanctuary.

Jewish Response

The synagogue serves many functions within the Jewish community. It is a Beit Tefilah (house of prayer) where Jews come together as a community to worship. It is a Beit Midrash (house of study) where Jewish education is offered from preschool, day school, and supplemental schools to adult education. It is a Beit Knesset (house of assembly) where groups of people come together and participate in programs relating to the holidays, the environment, social justice, family issues, entertainment and more.

Muslim Response

Muslims worship in a mosque (also called a masjid). Mosques vary in size and shape throughout the world—ranging from grand structures with large domes and tall slender towers (called minarets)—to small structures or even an individual room within a building. Muslims gather at mosques for Friday prayers, as well as daily prayers. Mosques often serve as community centers, as well, offering a place for Muslims to meet with each other. Although it is preferable to worship together in a mosque, a Muslim may pray almost anywhere, such as in streets, offices, schools or factories.

✡ Evan, age 8

Our Holy Books

Christian Response

The Bible for Christians consists of two sections: The Old Testament (all those books written before Jesus was born) and the New Testament (those books which tell the stories of Jesus' life and teachings and tell of life after his death). Christians receive instructions for living faithful lives in the words found in the Bible. Another way to think of the Old and New Testaments is the Hebrew Bible and the Christian Bible.

Jewish Response

The Torah (Hebrew for "the teachings") is the name given to the five books of Moses: Genesis, Exodus, Leviticus, Numbers and Deuteronomy, which come at the very beginning of the Jewish Bible, which also includes the Prophets and the Writings. The Jewish Bible is called Tanakh. These books are the core of Jewish law and practice, as well as Jewish history. Each week in synagogues throughout the world, the same section of the Torah is read out loud to the congregation, as well as a section from the Prophets. Rabbi Hillel, of the First Century BCE, said that the main idea of the Torah is "What is hateful to you, do not do to your neighbor." This concept is what leads us to acts of loving kindness and tzedakah (righteousness).

Muslim Response

The Holy Qur'an ("Koo-rahn"), which Muslims believe to be the word of God, is the Muslim holy book. The Qur'an contains 114 chapters that were revealed to the Prophet Muhammad (one of several Prophets, but is considered the Prophet of Islam) during his lifetime. The words of the Qur'an were passed on to the followers of Prophet Muhammad (Muslims) orally until the Qur'an was recorded in a written form a short time after his death. The Qur'an contains many of the same stories found in the Old Testament. In addition to the Holy Qur'an, Muslims also seek guidance from examining the sayings and practices of the Prophet Mohammed during his lifetime. These sayings and practices are recorded in narrations known as hadith.

How We Pray

Christian Response

Christians pray the Lord's Prayer in unison (a prayer Jesus taught when asked how to pray). They also pray in private in their own way. And when a congregation prays together (often led by the pastor), people's concerns and celebrations are shared with God. Prayer is considered a personal conversation with God. For some, prayers are shared while kneeling or closing one's eyes or bowing one's head in reverence.

Jewish Response

Jewish worship includes private prayer, as well as rituals that are observed in the home, like lighting candles at the beginning of Shabbat (the Jewish Sabbath). It also emphasizes communal prayer. Some Jewish people worship at three services a day and a fourth on Shabbat, which occurs from sundown Friday night until sundown Saturday. Other Jewish people worship primarily on Shabbat. Prayers are recited in Hebrew and in English, both sung and recited. Prayer services are lead by the Rabbi (teacher) and the Chazzan (cantor).

Muslim Response

Prayer is a very important part of the daily lives of Muslims. Salah is the name for the obligatory prayers that are performed five times a day, and are a direct link between the worshipper and God. They are performed at dawn, noon, the afternoon, sunset, and nighttime. Prayers contain verses from the Qur'an ("Koo-rahn") and are said in Arabic, the language of God's revelation. Personal supplications, or prayers, however, can be offered in one's own language and at any time. These five daily prayers can be performed individually or communally. Fridays are considered the "holy day" where Muslims pray communally—with Friday prayer preceded by a short sermon from the prayer leader called an imam ("ih-mahm"). During prayer, Muslims stand shoulder to shoulder and kneel to the ground a number of times, depending on which prayer is being performed. All Muslims pray in one direction, toward the Holy Kaaba in the city of Mecca. It is important for Muslims to be physically and spiritually clean and pure while performing prayer, so Muslims will perform a ritual washing before praying.

What We Eat and Drink

Jewish Response

The Jewish people have lots of delicious foods that are associated with holidays and life cycle events. Wine (in moderation) is a symbol of joy and the holiness of time and freedom. Jewish people who observe the kosher laws do not eat certain foods like pork and shellfish. There are many other rules and customs associated with keeping kosher. Jewish food comes from all over the world. Recipes range from spicy Yemenite and Syrian treats, to the classic chicken soup and latkes (potato pancakes) of Eastern Europe. The braided challah, which is made with eggs, is the special Shabbat and holiday bread.

Muslim Response

Muslims around the world follow a few dietary restrictions throughout the year. Muslims are forbidden from eating pork or drinking alcohol. Food that is permissible for Muslims to eat is termed halal, similar to the idea of kosher in the Jewish faith. For meat to be considered halal, the animal needs to be treated humanely before being butchered while invoking the name of God. Since Islam is found in many countries and cultures across the globe, there is no particular food that is common to the Muslim faith. During the holy month of Ramadan, Muslims will often gather to break the daily fast communally, traditionally with dates and water or milk. The main meal that follows (called an Iftar) is typically reflective of the local cultural cuisine.

✡Evan, age 8

Our Important Days and Holidays

Anonymous

Christian Response

The two most important holidays ("holy days") for a Christian are Christmas and Easter. Christmas is the celebration of Jesus' birth. It is always on December 25th. Easter is the celebration of His resurrection after death. Good Friday is the day we remember His death on a cross. These days mark the end of Lent which is a 40-day period to remember when Jesus was in the desert preparing for ministry and being tempted. The dates for these vary each year and fall sometime between February and April. There are many other special days, including Ash Wednesday, Pentecost, and All Saints Day, but Christmas and Easter are the most important.

Jewish Response

The rhythm of Jewish life is determined by its calendar. There are rituals, celebrations and holidays that are observed on a daily, weekly, monthly and yearly basis. Most important is Shabbat, beginning at sundown on Friday and ending at sundown on Saturday. Shabbat is meant to be a day of rest or peace. Some Jewish people observe Shabbat by refraining from working, using electricity, carrying things and more. Others observe Shabbat as a gift of time, to be with family, to share a time of joy, to enjoy good food, and be with good friends.

Here are a few other important Jewish Holidays:
- Rosh Hashanah is the Jewish New Year
- Yom Kippur is the Day of Atonement
- Sukkot is the Harvest Festival and Feast of Booths
- Chanukah is the Festival of Lights, celebrating the Jewish victory over the Greek oppressors
- Passover is the Festival of our Freedom (from slavery)

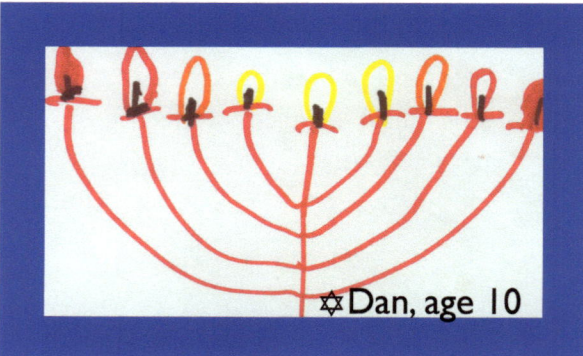
Dan, age 10

Muslim Response

All Muslims celebrate two main holidays: Eid Al-Fitr and Eid Al-Adha. The holy month of Ramadan is also an important time of the year, though not a holiday. Since Muslim holidays follow the lunar calendar, these holidays do not fall on a fixed date, but instead vary each year. Eid Al-Fitr is a three-day holiday to mark the end of the holy month of Ramadan. During Ramadan, the ninth month of the Islamic calendar, Muslims from all continents unite in a period of fasting (refrain from food and water from dawn until sunset). This is a month of spiritual reflection and self-purification; it also helps teach us self-restraint and patience, and helps us realize our blessings.

Precious, age 7

Eid Al-Adha is a four day holiday that Muslims celebrate to honor the Prophet Abraham's willingness to sacrifice his son Ishmael as an act of obedience to God. God substituted a lamb in Ishmael's place, so as a result Muslims will typically sacrifice a lamb during this holiday, offering the meat to the poor and to their neighbors. Eid Al-Adha also marks the return of Muslims performing their pilgrimage to Mecca. The pilgrimage to Mecca (the hajj) is an obligation for all Muslims in their lifetime. Each year, over two million people from every corner of the globe meet in Mecca, Saudi Arabia providing a unique opportunity for those of different nations to meet one another. The annual hajj begins in the twelfth month of the Islamic year.

Faith Partners who have participated in Peace by Piece:

American Muslim Interactive Network
Baltimore Hebrew Congregation
Chizuk Amuno Congregation
Christian Temple
Johns Hopkins University Muslim Student Association
First Christian Church
The Gathering
Mt. Olivet Christian Church
St. Andrews
Civic Works
Elijah Cummings Youth Program

First and St. Stephen's United Church of Christ
Har Sinai Congregation
Islamic Society of Baltimore
    Al Rahma and An Nur Mosques
Kol Halev Congregation
Maryland Province Jesuits
    Loyola University Maryland Campus Ministry
    Loyola University Maryland Center for Community Service & Justice
Masjid Al-Inshirah
Morgan State- Muslim Student Association
Muslim Community Cultural Center
Progressive Muslim Network
St. Paul's School
St. Timothy's School

A special thanks to those who have contributed to make this book possible...

American Muslim Interactive Network
Baltimore Hebrew Congregation
Chizuk Amuno Congregation
Christian Temple
Elijah Cummings Youth Program
Muslim Community Cultural Center
St. Paul's School
Jayna Powell
Rebecca Dulka

Habitat for Humanity of the Chesapeake is a 501(c)(3) nonprofit registered in the State of Maryland.

Apprentice House is the country's only campus-based, student-staffed book publishing company. Directed by professors and industry professionals, it is a nonprofit activity of the Communication Department at Loyola University Maryland.

Using state-of-the-art technology and an experiential learning model of education, Apprentice House publishes books in untraditional ways. This dual responsibility as publishers and educators creates an unprecedented collaborative environment among faculty and students, while teaching tomorrow's editors, designers, and marketers.

Outside of class, progress on book projects is carried forth by the AH Book Publishing Club, a co-curricular campus organization supported by Loyola University Maryland's Office of Student Activities.

Eclectic and provocative, Apprentice House titles intend to entertain as well as spark dialogue on a variety of topics. Financial contributions to sustain the press's work are welcomed. Contributions are tax deductible to the fullest extent allowed by the IRS.

To learn more about Apprentice House books or to obtain submission guidelines, please visit www.ApprenticeHouse.com.

Apprentice House
Communication Department
Loyola University Maryland
4501 N. Charles Street
Baltimore, MD 21210
Ph: 410-617-5265 • Fax: 410-617-2198
info@apprenticehouse.com

www.ingramcontent.com/pod-product-compliance
Lightning Source LLC
Chambersburg PA
CBHW042031150426
43199CB00003B/24